EXPOSING HIS SECRET

Twelve Years of Child Sexual Abuse

Carrie D Darlyn

ISBN: 0692845755
ISBN 13: 9780692845752

FOREWORD

By Shelley Saffer, Rockchester, NY

2 Corinthians 1:3- 7 "Praise be to the God and Father of our Lord Jesus Christ, the Father of compassion and the God of all comfort, [4] who comforts us in all our troubles, so that we can comfort those in any trouble with the comfort we ourselves receive from God. [5] For just as we share abundantly in the sufferings of Christ, so also our comfort abounds through Christ. [6] If we are distressed, it is for your comfort and salvation; if we are comforted, it is for your comfort, which produces in you patient endurance of the same sufferings we suffer. [7] And our hope for you is firm, because we know that just as you share in our sufferings, so also you share in our comfort."

It was common practice to strip criminals when they were crucified, to expose them to humiliation. No doubt they were also beaten on their genitals as part of the standard cruelty to those being punished. Our Savior, therefore, no doubt experienced such abuse and could therefore identify with this aspect of human suffering as well.

There is nothing like hearing from someone who has BEEN THERE when you are going through or have been through such trauma as my sister in Christ has. She is open about her experiences and how the Lord brought her through and continues to help her deal with the long-lasting effects. Anyone who has endured sexual abuse can draw encouragement from her testimony here. Those who have been blessed not to go through such a trauma can learn something too, to keep their ears open to a child trying to say the unthinkable.

I pray this book would serve as a blessing and exhortation to all who read. Shelley Saffer

ACKNOWLEDGMENT

I want to express my great gratitude for God: my Father who has always been with me and given me strength and courage and who continues to help me through the rough times in my life come what may. He has never failed me or left me alone. I am thankful that He will never fail me.

In addition, I want to thank my dear husband and children for their love and understanding through thick and thin. They have had to deal with the aftermath of my childhood ordeal, which has been quite severe and not fair to them. I am so thankful for all my friends and church family who has prayed for me faithfully not even knowing what great help they supplied.

Last but not least, I would like to thank my editor, Billy Van. He graciously volunteered to edit for me. He is a hard worker and an accomplished writer. I appreciate his hard work of carefully editing my work. This is my first book and I am sure that caused his work to be a challenge. Without the editor my work would be very raw. My words flowed as I wrote them down but that is different in the finished product. Billy caused my manuscript to flow through the stories more like a book should. I am thankful for people, like Billy, who still want to help others. I will always be grateful to him for his help.

DEDICATION

I dedicate this book to all of the children, male and female, that has had and also is having to endure such an injustice of child sexual abuse. There is so much loss to those precious children and betrayal of authority by the adult perpetrators involved. My heart breaks because of these horrible things thrust upon those innocent human beings who want so much to love and please and just be loved. Such evil in this world, I know, goes on every single day without fail. My sincere desire is to let victims know they are not alone, and they are not at fault for any reason. God loves each of us with an everlasting love. Even though these things, in my opinion, are some of the most horrendous evils, God is not to blame. Human beings are given the free will to choose to do evil or good. In my opinion, the whole Bible instructs us how to learn God's ways and tells us the consequences of choosing to live sinful, evil lives. Our choices affect not only ourselves, but also everyone around us unfortunately.

I want to let every victim and survivor know that you can get through this. Please, please, please tell someone, and if that person does not listen tell someone else. Keep telling until someone gets you out of that situation and environment. There is help out there.

CHILD ABUSE HOTLINE   24/7 CHILD HELP NATIONAL
1-800-4-A-CHILD
1-800-422-4453
http://www.childhelp.org/hotline

TABLE OF CONTENTS

1

THE RECURRING BATTLE INSIDE

I want to begin to explain the strange beginning to my story. Many, many times throughout adulthood, I have had things bothering me deep down in my core that I honestly could not figure out what was the matter with me. It sounds very unbelievable, even to myself that this happened every few years. I would finally, after some time had passed, make an appointment with the psychiatrist that I began seeing for therapy since I was about 23 years old. I had so much depression that for many years I wished I had never been born. I had often thought of ways to kill myself but never attempted anything. But after my session with the doctor began, the root of my problem hit me right in the face...again and again.

In 2013, I was having these same feelings and began to journal again because that seems to help. I felt sure it was not the abuse crushing me this time but I was wrong—it was, and in a few pages you will read where I saw the truth. I felt sure that since I had forgiven my father I was done with it. *(I prefer not to call him daddy for sure. It takes a special man to be a daddy. Usually I call him dad but prefer just "he or him".)* The forgiving has been a long hard process for me because of the fact the abuse was not believed by anyone or was not validated or admitted, where it counted at least. He was not punished for it. In truth, I don't know why. Anyway, the reason my story begins like this is because I've always wanted to write a book to help someone else and did not know how. So, I decided to use my journal not only for helping explore my tangled feelings, but helping me attempt to write my book. The memories and words flowed like a stream in the journal. I was hoping I could accomplish my goal through this method.

Let me explain my problem: My own flesh and blood father, from the age of three or four years old until I was fifteen, sexually abused me. I have never, even to this day, understood why. He was not drunk when the incidents occurred. He never admitted it where it counted and NEVER said he was sorry. He did admit it one single time. One point in time when I was nine or ten years old, he got a job about 50 miles north and so did my mother. They employed a fifteen-year-old-babysitter to sit with us three kids when they both were at work. One day there must have been a gap when it was not time for him to leave and mom was already at work and the babysitter was there. I remember playing out in the yard on the swing set that day when the babysitter came over to me asked me point blank if 'he' ever touched me in bed. My mouth flew open and my head dropped as I asked her "why?". She proceeded to tell me that he had told her that I '*let*' him do things to me in bed. You see, he was trying to talk her into having sex with him. I told her the true story of what was going on. She believed me! We never saw her again after that day.

I was always trying to get him to admit what was going on by writing him notes and saying little things here and there. I even told him that I forgave him. I so wanted him to get saved. In addition, I told him that he must forgive himself. All these things occurred after I had been married for several years.

I want everyone whom I can reach to know and realize the extent of damage this kind of abuse does to a child. It does not go away. It gets easier to handle with God's help and therapy...and believe me, it has taken me 46 years working and trying to understand how with God's help to really feel like I have completely forgiven him.

He got lung cancer when he was 61 years old and passed away that next year at the age of 62. Praise God he did get saved and I was so glad, but still he did not apologize to me. He never admitted it. He never did anything to help me. That was so important to me, but it never happened and I had to forgive him for that also.

August 9th, 2013 (From my Journal)
As I lie here in bed, I feel really disgusted once again about my weight. Of all the diets I have been on in my lifetime, now I can't seem to make one work. I went back on Weight Watcher points plus and I've gained 2 lbs. I have been on it for a couple weeks this time and I can't seem to stay on track long enough to lose. It is so hard to do to resist all the sweets and resist eating my fill, wherein lies my problem.

The first psychiatrist I went to for anxiety and depression told me that over-eating was self-rewarding. I know now that this is true, although at the time I really felt angry when he told me that. I would like to know why I am rewarding myself.

All this rewarding has resulted in hurting my health and self es-teem. The awful thing about it though is that I can't seem to stop. It seems like a huge addiction and a vicious circle. The more emotional pain and stress I experience, the more I want to eat. The more I eat, the more I feel shame and emotional strain because of it. I can't count the times I have asked God to help me with this unhealthy relationship with food. I can tell you that He always answers those prayers. Then I stop listening to His voice and end up relapsing. God is faithful and never leaves us; on the contrary WE do the leaving.

One more idea I always think about is that I believe losing weight does not HAVE to include not enjoying your food, otherwise why

God would have given us taste buds to experience the good taste of food?

Dear Lord, Life as I know it is so, so stressful these days. You know I've been through many days of stress similar to this and I also know that everyone else has his or her own stress to deal with and I am not the only one. God, I am so thankful that I do not have to take this journey of life alone. Thank You for saving my soul and for being my constant companion and friend, for bailing me out of so many messes and for loving me despite all my sins and failures. Thank You for my dear husband, who stands by me through the good times and the bad. I love him, I love You.

Saturday Night, August 10th, 2013
Needing to get my priorities straight is what God is dealing with me about right now. Missing church is really bothering me. I miss my church family. I miss being among my brothers and sisters in Christ and feeding off God's Holy Spirit that I feel in that environment. The Spirit flows through the singing, praying, the fellowship, and the reading of God's Holy Word and learning about it during the services. Then when I have the privilege of singing for Him and to Him, He blesses me so much. I love to praise and worship God because of His great goodness and mercy.

I've been having migraines on the Sundays that I don't have to work, then on the Sundays I do have to work I am not able to fall asleep until 5 AM, then I cannot get up and go on those days either. Please Lord, help my feet calm down and my migraines hold off until after church somehow so that I can get back into church regularly again. Help me try harder to go even when I don't feel like it. Forgive me for my failures; help me keep my eyes on You. Thank You for blessing us. I love You.

Thursday, September 12th, 2013

It's been about a month since my last journal entry. Thank You Lord for answering my prayer! Praise You God for You are worthy! My migraines have let up, and this week (we had revival at church Sun through Wed) September 9, 10, and 11. I have made it to church Sunday, Monday, and Tuesday! I sang *God on the Mountain* Sunday morning and Tuesday night and by request using Soundtrack music as I often do. Many requests were made, so I know God is speaking to people through the song and my prayer is to stay out of the way and let God speak and bless through the vessel (me). I am so blessed and honored to be able to do this for Him. Thank You Lord for allowing me to share with others how good You are in my life by means where they listen and really hear Your message. I was so humbled to hear that a seven-year-old boy wants to bring his IPAD and video me singing it because he loves the song so much. Oh, dear God please keep Your hands on the precious youngsters attending our church. Lead them where they will never be able to learn enough about You and will love You and serve You always. Hold them close to Your side, and please stay close to my blessed granddaughter. Lord, please be with her especially through these teenage years. Help her know how precious she is to You. Lead her in the path she should go and let her love and serve You always.

Lord, help me learn to know the right things to say in public—to be tactful and courteous, without judging—and to know when not to say anything. I never learned how to really act among people in public. I desperately need Your help. I don't know how to say things accurately and Lord I need to stop using those not so nice words that the enemy assures that won't hurt to say. It's like a part of me is trying to be like the world but I don't feel that You are pleased with that and neither am I. Please forgive me and help me stop. Most of all, help me have a forgiving heart and attitude. I want to do everything I do with love and say everything I say with love and kindness. I want to be more like You. I love You, Lord.

September 22-23, 2013; 2:00 AM

Some things happened tonight and my reaction, comments, and attitude were not pleasing to me and I know not pleasing to You, Lord. A situation at work tonight where a CNA didn't get her charting done and I was required to stay until it was completed, frustrated me greatly. The reason I was frustrated so much is because she seemed to not take the charting seriously after another CNA and I told her that the charting had to be done before she left work. I told her I would help her (she was a new employee) but that she needed to learn to chart as she went and not wait until the end of the shift to do it all. I expressed my unhappiness to have to stay until it was done along with her. Was I too harsh with her? I wish I had chosen my words more carefully and been a little gentler…maybe. I don't know, but I do know another CNA had to chart for her a few nights ago plus got her own charting done. Then to top things off, she left without telling me she was leaving and her charting was only 77% rather than 100% complete. It took me about ten minutes to look the building over for her and then found out she was gone and left all the rest of her charting for me to complete! Was she just too overwhelmed? I hope I didn't cause her to give up and give her the impression that I wouldn't work with her.

Lord, I just don't like how my mouth is saying things about others—even though the things may be true. I don't think I should be saying negative things about others. I don't like it. Please, just help me stop. Help me to always act like Your child. I am embarrassed, to say the least. I admit I do not know how to act in public—I beg You, Lord, to please teach me to bridle my tongue, my selfish thoughts, and act and talk in ways pleasing to You—forever Yours through Christ my Savior.

Monday morning 2:25 AM September 23, 2013
I have thoughts of my Christian life down through the years and it seems like I have progressed so slowly. I attribute a large portion of it due to my selfishness, stubbornness, and earthly mindedness. I wish I had had a closer relationship to the Lord, read my Bible so much more, studied it more, prayed more, and obeyed the Word more. My prayer this minute is: Dear Lord, Praise and glory are given to Your name. I believe Your word and truth more than ever before. Please make my mind and heart absorb Your laws and Your word and Your ways like a dry sponge absorbs water. Help me be saturated with Your love for others, Your laws and ways because I know they are right. Please give me Your eyes to see and understand. Guide me into right living. Help me hate lying and evil more and more. I love You. You are worthy of all praise and glory!

October 20, 2013; Sunday night @ 1:00 AM
I wanted to jot down a few things. First, the One who made heaven and earth has spoken to my spirit about the truth and His ways. According to the world, one must give in to today's compromises and way of doing things to get by. Things like lying; I don't know why a person would have to lie, cheat, steal, etc, to make things work even in the business world. Uprightness and truth is what is needed to succeed!

Lord, teach me to live by Your precepts, Your laws no matter what. Help me.

I love You, Lord. Thank You for all my blessings and so much help.

November 23, 2013; Saturday
On the front cover of my journal I wrote the words "Thoughts of my life through the years" because I wanted to have something to go by to write my life story. Every time I pick up this journal to write in it, I

read the front and realize I haven't really written things that deal with the past years, just things happening now. Well, I am going to try to do both from now on.

First, thoughts about my weight throughout the years and my relationship with food come to mind. I realized today how I've been overweight most of my adult life. When I have lost weight I haven't kept it off for very long except for the last time. I lost 100 lbs beginning 2004 and reached my goal of 114 lbs in August 2008. I kept it off for three years for the first time in thirty-seven years. I was so happy about that and proud, although God did the strength giving and gave me the determination and motivational tools to do it. I should not have been proud, I don't think, because God resists the proud. Next time I will just be thankful to Him! Anyway, I was just so happy that I had lost the weight and to have kept it off that long.

I began gaining back those lost pounds that third year (2011) at Christmas and Thanksgiving dinners. Ongoing treats and the extra weight I picked up didn't come off like it did the previous two years. Then I lost my mom in 2009 and it was hard not to eat more during the grieving process. After all that, I had to go back to work in January of 2012. I didn't have the time or energy to fight the weight gain after that. I was really disgusted with myself because I said I would never gain that weight again. I haven't given up yet, though. I am still trying to lose the weight again. Thanksgiving of 2013 I weighed 175. *(I got back up to 192 lbs in 2014. With God's help, I lost down to 184 now and I am still trying to lose more.)* Please, help me, Lord. I love You.

November 27, 2013: 2:02 AM
I feel so ashamed because I threw a temper tantrum at work tonight. I filled in for another staff nurse and worked an extra shift on my day off and got stuck with a hall I did not want to work. It was a hard section of the facility to work, but I acted like a spoiled brat and not at all how I believe God wanted me to behave. The battle inside me did

not feel Christ-like at all. I am unhappy with myself for all the awful and mean thoughts that sailed through my head. The point is that my whole life is filled with these wars inside my mind wanting to lash out at others with such rage that would not fix the problem but only hurt others and not only that but would be a great hindrance to pointing others to Christ in any way, shape, or form. I do not want to feel this way. I do not want to be this way.

I love my Lord so much and I want to be more like Him and walk in His ways by showing more godly love and give hope to the hopeless.

Strangely, but should not seem so, there is a bright side to this whole thing. I could feel God's presence though I did not feel worthy of it. I heard His voice through His word. It was like an amplified example of Romans 7:14-25 (*"So the trouble is not with the law, for it is spiritual and good. The trouble is with me, for I am all too human, a slave to sin. I don't really understand myself, for I want to do what is right, but I don't do it. Instead, I do what I hate. But if I know that what I am doing is wrong, this shows that I agree that the law is good. So I am not the one doing wrong; it is sin living in me that does it. And I know that nothing good lives in me, that is, in my sinful nature. I want to do what is right, but I can't. I want to do what is right, but I don't. I don't want to do what is wrong, but I do it anyway. But if I do what I don't want to do, I am not really the one do-ing wrong; it is sin living in me that does it. I have discovered this principle of life—that when I want to do what is right, I inevitably do what is wrong. I love God's law with all my heart. But there is another power within me that is at war with my mind. This power makes me a slave to the sin that is still within me. Oh, what a miserable person I am! Who will free me from this life that is dominated by sin and death? Thank God! The answer is in Jesus Christ our Lord. So you see how it is; In my mind I really want to obey God's law, but because of my sinful nature I am a slave to sin."NLT*) This is the way I feel for real! I wanted to just throw myself down on my knees and let Jesus take full control, but I felt so weak. I was working so I couldn't do it, but if I could have I would have.

But tonight I feel like God has taught me that when I am weak, He is strong and that He still loves me and cares how I grow in His grace even with all my quirks and flaws in my flesh.

My sister, who works here too, brought me over a rosebud before she left for home. That rose reminded me of how blessed I am of God's beauty and how He makes all things work together for good. It also reminded me to focus on the good things in life, and love, and peace. Thank you, Lord from my whole heart.

"Don't let evil conquer you, but conquer evil by doing good"

NLT. Romans 12:21

2

THE REVELATION

November 27th, 2013; 11:59 PM (Still noting from my journal)

Tonight my husband and I began talking about an abusive husband, who held his wife hostage, threatened her many times at gunpoint. He had been drugging her, brainwashing her and more. He would pull her hair, hit her, push her, and scream as loudly as he could an inch from her face. Her hearing has been permanently damaged because of that. She did get away from him and get a divorce thank the Lord.

He was sexually abusing his own daughter, and had in fact sexually abused his stepdaughter while his daughter helplessly watched. The law won't prosecute him. He lies his way out of everything. There are numerous evil things this man has done and yet he seems to get away with it. I became very angry as I thought about these precious lives destroyed by someone who seems to enjoy his ability to make others miserable.

The rage turned two fold when I began thinking of my own past and what my own father put me through. I didn't even realize but in fact here it is once again for me to deal with at 60 years old. Numerous times since I began treatment for the damage caused by this monster, I would feel fine and then something inside of me began to rage. I would lash out at other people, become angry and cry for no apparent reason. Many other symptoms would surface just like this time, having nightmares when I could sleep and insomnia at other times. It would not dawn on me that it was the monster causing all these things to happen to me until a month or so of being miserable and not knowing why. I, to this day, do not understand why I don't immediately know what is going on when it happens.

I've had so many lasting effects caused by this trauma in my life. I have nightmares…. horrible nightmares where I wake up screaming. For a very long time I had what is called 'flashbacks', where I saw and felt the same things as when the abuse was happening. Usually, a certain word or specific place I saw or something similar triggered the flashbacks. I have had very low self-esteem and major depression. I have had many unhealthy thoughts, deep depression, loss of interest in everyday life, crying spells, feelings of worthlessness, and other such symptoms. I would not be emotionally available for my two girls many times in their childhood because of the effects left by the abuse. I wanted to stop all the abuse in <u>my</u> generation. I tried so hard to make sure my girls were not treated the way I was treated. What I did not realize until later was that those horrid side effects were causing my life to be so abnormal that my children would not have a normal childhood either because of me. That is a fact that one doesn't fully see until after it is done. The sins of one person do not stop at that person because the effects of those wrong decisions made by him affect everyone around him. The Bible warns of what sin does to not only the one sinning, but how it affects future generations. I decided that I could only do the very best I could with what I had been left. I was heartbroken just to say the least. I know in my heart that God is God in the good times and also in the bad. He makes good come from bad circumstances.

I had a family portrait that belonged to my mother hanging on my living room wall. The picture was of my parents and my brother, sister, and me. I was in my thirties when this picture was taken and I did not think it would bother me to leave it there after my mother passed away in 2009 (*we had previously bought her house and she lived with us so most of the pictures hanging were hers*). After I finally figured out the problem I knew it was the picture that had triggered this fit of rage and I had to remove it from my wall and put it away. I knew because of the way I felt every time I saw it, even out of the corner of my eye.

What an impact one person can have on another's life, especially on a child's life. After all these years I still have flashbacks and night-mares about certain incidents of what happened to me. Most people could not imagine all the awful things that I experienced beginning at the age of three or four years old. My own brother six years young-er than me did not even know this abuse happened even though he lived in the same household. When I first told him it happened, he said, "No". It took a time before he could understand that what I told was the truth. He believes me now. It is going on in countless homes today to children right under their sibling's nose and they have no clue. The perpetrators are very cunning and know how to make kids keep their secret. They are intimidating and threatening. They know that children will be afraid of them. In many cases, just like mine, even if they do tell nothing will be done. People do not like to talk about this subject. It is very hard to prove and the perpetrators do not look like bad people. Other people did not see him behind closed doors. This man on the outside seemed a very nice man, very intel-ligent, hard working, and good looking to everyone on the other side of that door. On the inside of him however, this man ruled with an iron fist. He was the boss and in no uncertain terms. He was going to get what he wanted and every member of this family would obey his orders. I lived this way until I married and moved out.

After I graduated high school, I got a job. I didn't get to keep any money from working though. He informed me when I received my first paycheck that I would give the money to him because he was laid off from work. My mother was working too at the time, so I did not understand why I had to give him all the money. My thoughts and opinions did not matter; I had to do what I was told. The fact is that I wouldn't have minded at all to contribute to family expenses, but thought it was too much for him to take everything. I tried to move away but that didn't work either. I called a lawyer out of the yellow pages of the phone book the day I turned eighteen. I asked the attorney at what age a person was legally an adult. He told me eighteen. I questioned him carefully because I knew what the tyrant would tell me. He assured me that my parents could not legally control me at my current age. I immediately told the iron fist that I was going to move. The first thing out of his mouth was that I was too young. When I informed him of the information I had just obtained from the attorney, he just went ballistic! He threatened to "stomp me into the floor", and beat me until I couldn't walk. He then instructed my mother, brother, and sister that they were to keep their eyes on me at all times. I was not allowed to talk to or see my boyfriend and I was a literal prisoner for two weeks. I was not so worried about myself but I was afraid of what he might do to my boyfriend if I did leave. How I wanted to leave...

Anyway, I didn't leave. That incident caused trauma too. It caused me to feel like someone had tied me up and held me down and I was helpless. I could not stand for anyone to even play like they were holding onto me where I felt in any way restrained. For years and years, I felt like I couldn't breathe and had anxiety attacks whenever that happened.

I am ashamed to say that after I married my boyfriend, I did not leave and never return. I felt lost, alone, and unable to function much of the time. I was never allowed to go to social functions at school such as ballgames growing up. I was not allowed to go to parties or associate with friends away from school. The truth is that I didn't know how to live in the real world. I could not understand why I behaved that way and stayed around and acted like nothing happened just like everyone else.

Moreover, one Father's Day I wrote this poem for his gift from me because we didn't have the money to buy him anything. I tried and tried so hard to forgive and act as though I was okay. In fact, I went too far the other way, pretending that the relationship was normal. I left out all the horrors of the abuse. I guess I wanted a father/daughter relationship so badly, I would try anything to get him to understand and love me the way he should have loved his daughter....God's way. The poem went like this:

> Today is Father's Day it's true. A day that's special, just for you.
> I think of all the words I'll say to tell you in a different way.
> Of how much I love you; how much I care.
> And when I need you, you are there.
> You've worked so hard your whole life through.
> You knew there were things you had to do.
> To provide us with things like shoes, food and a bed.
> And from these responsibilities you didn't turn your head.
> There are those who just go their own way,
> And let their families go where they may.
> The choice is ours as to what we will do.
> I'm so glad God gave me you.
> You gave me love down through the years,
> And though there were times there might have been tears,
> All of the good things out weigh the bad.
> I'm so glad God made you my dad.
> I love you very much,
> Your daughter, Shirley

Somehow in my mind my earthly father was two parts of a man or personality if you will. It may have been one of the coping mechanisms within me. On the one hand was the bad part and on the other side was a 'good' part in that he worked and provided for our family. I was told his education consisted of only finishing 3rd grade. Yet, he built several houses for our family, one of which was a very nice brick house. He was unable to read but he held jobs of mechanics, diesel and gas engine repairs, logging, coal mining, etc. I don't understand why but I was actually proud of him for his accomplishments in those areas. I feel like I should have hated every part of him. Truly I believe God and His holy word allowed me to see some good in him. The scriptures tell us to honor our parents. I suppose only God understands why we act and feel the way we do. I wanted to please my Heavenly Father so very much. No matter what a body goes through in this world that is evil, I know that God is pleased if the intentions of our heart are to please Him. God is a good, good Father and has no bad or evil side. I know He was always with me helping me cope and get through this life. I love Him with all of my heart and being. I wasn't perfect and made so many mistakes. Praise God though, He covered me with His precious blood and in the end the bad part of my earthly father was also covered by the saving blood of Christ. Only God my good Father could help me have this attitude. For this I am forever truly thankful.

I always wondered why all of him could not have been like this half. I longed for a full fledged dad and not the half dad, half monster that I had and tried my hardest to change....tried my hardest to be good enough....tried my hardest to figure out why......

As I mentioned, I was ashamed because I didn't disown my parents after I had married. I didn't understand why I couldn't do it when finally I could have. When I went into the hospital some years later for two weeks of intensive therapy for *Survivors of Child Sexual Abuse*, the therapists told us that behavior such as this is common among survivors. The term they used was "meshed" relationships where unhealthy bonds were more than bonds and very difficult to change. In addition I was diagnosed with PTSD at that time.

I did tell my perpetrator that if he did anything to **my** children that I would put him in prison and that he had better not touch them inappropriately. I meant that too! To the best of my knowledge, he never did touch them inappropriately.

Consider this question for yourself. I could never even imagine why this would happen. What would possess a grown man of 26 years old to even think of forcing little more than a toddler to perform sexual acts on him, let alone doing it? What pleasure could a grown man get from that? Nevertheless, he used this innocent child for sexual pleasuring of himself, although the reasoning of these acts escapes me completely.

3

IN THE BEGINNING

I remember the very first time something happened that didn't feel right soon after he was discharged from the army. Mom was getting us all ready for bed and I had just had my bath and I had a flannel robe on and nothing else, but it was closed with a tie. I went to say goodnight to dad. He was sitting at the kitchen table and as I went to hug and kiss him he untied my belt and opened my robe and looked at my naked body. I was small, not more than four years old, but still embarrassed. I remember looking at him so surprised. You see, I was so elated that he was home from the army. He had written to my mom and told her that he was not going to get to come home on leave but I don't remember why. We all were heartbroken. I had seen one of my aunts praying because she was staying with my mom, my sister, and me. She was an avid churchgoer and often I went with her. So, I went into the bedroom and knelt on the floor next to our bed and asked God to please let my daddy come home. I promptly marched into the living room and told my mother that daddy would be home in three days. God answered that prayer to everyone's amazement except for mine!

Anyway, when he looked up and saw my expression, he whispered, "It's mine anyway". I didn't even know what he meant by that remark. I soon found out however. I remember one morning mom was in the kitchen cooking breakfast and I went in their bedroom where he still lay in bed. I jumped up into bed with him not expecting what followed. He tied a white handkerchief around my eyes. (He always carried one in his pants pocket). Then he said, "You better not tell momma or I'll whip you". Then he pushed me down in the bed under the sheet and put his private part in my mouth. It made me feel so awful. I had never seen a penis before, didn't even know what it was called but there I lay with a blindfold on my eyes and something big and awful in my mouth. I felt so creepy and I knew this was not right. I could not understand why he did it. He was discharged from the army a year or so later. The same act resumed and it happened again and again as the years went by. At some point he changed where he did a 'mock intercourse' but I don't remember when that happened. Thank God he never penetrated. Usually it happened when my mom was gone somewhere or he would take me for a ride on his motorcycle and make a stop in a secluded place before taking me home.

Another particular incident I remember was when we were at my paternal grandparent's house and he called me into the bedroom right behind the kitchen. I so did not want to go because I knew what was going to happen but I was too afraid of him not to obey. I remember thinking, "why don't he do it to my sister instead and leave me alone?" That particular sister died a little while after that and I always felt guilty for the thought. But, I was angry and embarrassed and hated what he was doing to me. I hated it so badly that I would try to think about other things and just tried so hard to not think about what was really happening while it was happening. It felt so "icky" and awful. Well, I *was* only seven, that's what God reminds me.

One other vivid memory of this happened when he took me for a motorcycle ride. I loved to ride motorcycles. He took me about a mile down the road and pulled over to a vacant lot where he proceeded to get me off the cycle and put down the kickstand. He sat down on the seat sideways and got out the handkerchief and tied it around my eyes. When it was over, I saw him wipe something off my shoe. I didn't even know what it was then. I was so small that day that I stood up in front of him and was just tall enough to do what was forced on me. It feels so sad to have your childhood and innocence stolen. For a long time I had bad flashbacks every time I passed that spot off the road. I also remember times when we lived at a different place and he had to take me to the bus stop in the car everyday when I had started first grade. We waited in the car every morning. What a great start to my day! NOT!!

After my sister passed away when I was eight years old, I remember living in a four-room shack that he had built. I dearly despised any time that my mother had to leave the three of us kids home alone with him. I lived in fear all the time that she would leave us or would die and leave us. They started talking about her getting a job. I hoped with everything inside of me that she would not. I did not want her to get a job. He wouldn't usually bother me if she were home. I do remember a couple of times the dirty deed was done when we lived there well enough to tell a little about them. Once it happened in the kitchen where he stood me up in a kitchen chair and tied up the handkerchief. The other time, I was terrified by a nightmare about being in a burning house. I was so afraid and my heart was pounding. I thought my momma slept on the side of the bed near the doorway but when I got there, I just wilted because it was he instead. I wished that I had just stayed in my own bed, but it was too late once he was awake, even with my mom on the other side of him in the same bed.

This abuse happened so many times that I cannot remember every incident, but I tried hard not to make the same mistake twice (like jumping in bed with him). It was very stressful to say the least. I worried about when it would happen again. I put my heart and soul into my schoolwork. I loved to go to school and I loved to learn. I tried very hard and made very good grades. I think that was one thing that kept me sane. After I got older though, like in eighth grade, I was so ashamed of what was happening. I thought something was surely wrong with me and I shuddered to even think of any of my schoolmates finding out the dirty secret that I was not supposed to tell momma. Moreover, I was afraid that the kids would make fun of me and think I was to blame. I sure did not want the kids at school to know.

One Christmas Eve we kids got our presents and then the adults were just sitting around talking. My mom called me over to her and asked me to do something that shocked me, even horrified me, just thinking about doing it. She told me to go over to my dad and whisper in his ear that he was the "greatest daddy in the world". I frantically thought to myself, 'If I do this he will think that I like what he is doing'; I absolutely hate what he is doing. I cannot possibly tell him this lie! What can I do? So, I decided that I would just go over and whisper in his ear, "I love you". That wasn't a lie. In spite of everything I hated about what he did and was doing to me, I loved him and I don't know why. I wanted him to be my daddy. I waited for him to stop doing those awful ugly shameful things to me and just love me. I didn't know why he was doing this to me. What did I do to cause it? Why didn't he love me like a daughter? My mother seemed to adore him. She did everything he told her to do. She always put him first, asked his permission for everything she did, so he must be okay and something is wrong with me. At least that's what I thought. I tried so hard to please both my parents. The most approval I got was when I made good grades at school. They both bragged on me to other people whenever I got my report card because I always got good grades. But nothing changed the awful things he did to me, no matter how good I tried to be. Somehow I knew the thing he was doing to me was meant for women who were wives.

I wanted so desperately to be just a little girl. When I was in first grade, we lived on what my mom called "the Woodson farm". It really didn't look like a farm to me but I didn't know what a farm was supposed to look like. It was there where he had to take me to the bus stop. Thankfully, I do have a few good memories of my life while living there. I remember we drank water from metal dippers. I learned at school that we should be wiping off the dipper after each one of us drank from it because of "germs". My parents were impressed when I told them about that! I was always trying to please by being "good" and making good grades. My eyes were feeling "funny" whenever I ate a meal. The plate and the food were always blurry and it made me dizzy and made my head hurt when I ate due to that. It turned out that I needed glasses. I had turned seven when I actually got them. My left eye was diagnosed as being "lazy". I had an Amblyopic left eye. I had to wear a patch over my good eye for a while. That was a miserable experience. I couldn't see very well at all with the right eye covered and I cried and cried until the eye doctor finally said he thought it was too late for the patch to work anyway so he discontinued it. I was so glad! I do remember when I got eyeglasses to help my vision, my dad said to me, "I didn't get these glasses just because you wanted them". Demeaning words hurt so badly at any age.

One morning my mom woke us kids up and told us a tornado passed by the night before. It had uprooted a huge tree in our back yard. I couldn't believe it. I had been playing in the mud right beside that big tree the day before and had made some perfectly wonderful "mud pies" which were still laying there!

One more thing I remember doing when we lived on the Woodson Farm and that was telling my first lie...intentionally. My parents were having another of their many arguments. It seems that mom had accused him of going out on her because...well, I don't know why. However, I had the day before had so much fun just writing on the family car in the dust. Somehow, the writing on the car became an issue in the argument. So, he said that I must have done it and called me outside to ask me if I in fact had done the writing. I wanted him to be in trouble and I felt this would be something I could do to help that happen, so I told them no, I did not write on the car. He begged and begged me to tell the truth. He told me, "You won't get in trouble if you did it but your momma thinks I went out on her." I insisted I did not do it no matter how hard he begged. I don't think I ever told them any differently. I know I should have told the truth because God is not pleased with lying. I AM sorry now, but I wasn't then.

Finally, the one very important detail that happened while we lived in that particular place, that was first time I told my mom what he had been doing to me. One hot summer day we all piled into the old family car and went to a mechanic shop where dad went to see about getting a job. Mom and we kids stayed in the car while he went into the shop to talk. We three kids were hot and fidgety and momma was just talking like she would talk to an adult. I, myself remember standing up in the back floorboard of the car, leaning on both elbows on the back of the front seat where mom and my little brother were sitting and I was very interested in what she was talking about. It seems there had been a rumor going around or it could have been a court trial going on, I don't remember which. Anyway, momma was talking about this local man that had molested his own daughter and mom made the comment that if, "her husband" ever done anything like that to one of her kids, she would have him arrested! Whew, I thought to myself, this is how I can get all this to stop! "Momma", I said. Daddy has done the same thing to me." You see, there were five people in our family and nobody as far as I know was aware of what was going on. Hiding those actions and keeping secrets were a specialty of the house. I know this because the look my mother gave me was one of complete shock and disbelief. She confronted him with the accusation and he promptly denied it. I guess my mom just thought that she was braver than she actually was or maybe she just didn't believe me because the police was never called and the abuse continued.

A while, maybe a couple of years later, my parents split up once again due to him going out with other women again. He would do that ever so often coupled with drinking while he was gone. On average, those sprees lasted about three days before he dragged himself back home. Anyway, we were at my maternal grandmother's house and they were still separated. I was actually happy when they were separated for obvious reasons and did not want them to get back together. One of the women he was cheating with just happened to be one of my mom's younger sisters. The word from her is that it did not last long because my deceased sister had appeared to the two of them while they were in the car one night and that spooked them enough that they broke off the relationship immediately. During that break up, I had broken my eyeglasses and mom was trying to get help to replace or repair them in which God provided help via the Lion's Club in our County. Aside from the fact that my mother was six years younger than my dad, had four, and then three children to care for did not make it easy for her to get out on her own. Times were different for those situations in the fifties and sixties. My mom was also a physical, verbal, and emotional abuse survivor herself and had all with which to deal. In addition, there was not as much help available in that time frame. I actually did not blame her at that time because I felt sorry for her. Her dad, I was told tried to push her and her mother down a flight of basement steps to kill them during a fight between her mom and dad. She was around seven or eight. I have noted that abuse begets abuse. My goal was to make it stop with <u>my</u> generation. I tried very very hard at that but the effects on the survivor of child sexual abuse makes it nearly impossible. Although, I did not abuse my children and tried to protect them from anyone abusing them, I was helpless when it came to my psychological condition resulting from so many years of sexual, verbal, and emotional abuse in my life. I found that I could not be the mom I wanted to be. I didn't know how to be normal, I had severe depression all of my adult life and looking back made so many mistakes because of it. I did the best I could with what I had to do with. God helped me with that. I am so, so thankful. I was far from perfect, but I tried to bring up my children in the love and admonition of the Lord. I took them to church and tried to live a life pleasing to God, as much as I was able in front of them. I was still so disappointed in myself.

4

THE SECOND AND THIRD TELLING

During this particular separation I remember my mom talking to my dad again and talking about reconciliation. I didn't want that to happen, so I told her again what he was continuing to do to me when we were alone together. I remember that she at least did call an attorney that time but had gotten information that there was little way to prove that he did what I accused him of doing unless I went to the doctor and the doctor found evidence by examination. Oh, how I didn't want that man doctor to look at me. She took me anyway but to my surprise, the doctor would not examine me because he stated that, "the evidence would be gone unless there was penetration and semen was deposited and left recently and that did not happen. The result of that was that once again, it was my word against his and my parents indeed went back together and the abuse resumed. My mom now told me that she did not want we kids to grow up without a father like she did. My mother's father died when my mother was eight, in an automobile accident on his way to work.

She didn't understand that we grew up without a "real father" even with him there. I myself was a sex toy instead of a daughter. The older I got the more I wanted to run away from home but I didn't know where I could go. The abuse went on. I remember the time my brother contracted hepatitis B and had to be hospitalized. I would say that I was about 12 years old at that time. I had decided in my own mind that it did no good to tell anymore but that didn't mean I wouldn't try my best not to be stuck alone with him without momma. Then something happened to change my mind about telling again…. I found out that he had been sexually abusing my little sister! I didn't care about myself as much but hurting her too was altogether a different story. So I told momma again and told about my sister too. So, I was told to stay with my brother at the hospital that night (a job I enjoyed!) while they hashed it out once again. My paternal grandmother said to my mother the next day when she and my mother and my sister got to the hospital where my brother and I waited for them, "If a child of mine would have told that on their daddy, I would have beaten their hides good!". I was standing right there when she said it and I was so devastated. I cried and cried and although they fought and argued, nothing was done. My depression had gotten so bad by the time I was 14 that my mother took me to her psychiatrist for an appointment. However, while we were in the waiting room waiting for the nurse to call me in to talk to the doctor, this is what my mother told me: "Don't you tell him what your daddy's done. If you do, he'll go to prison". At that moment I felt all hope drain from me. If I cannot tell what the problem is, how can I get anyone to help me? That was what my thoughts were. So, I went into the doctor's office and told him nothing.

The last time the act happened I just decided to fight back at least in a small way. He ordered my brother and sister to go outside and play and ordered me to stay in the house. I had been terrified that I would become pregnant with my own dad's baby because he had changed from oral sex to forcing me to lie still and he put his private between my legs. How humiliating it would have been to have my peers find out what was happening to me. So, anyway I told him that I didn't want to stay in the house with him. He said "well if you don't I'll just whip you with my belt". I said quickly, "Then whip me". But he forced me that day to lie down across the bed while he did the deed.

I would always keep my legs crossed as tightly as I possibly could so maybe I could prevent him penetrating me and me getting pregnant. I didn't want to have sex until my wedding night with my husband. Another day, soon after that one, he told me that he "didn't get finished". That's the day I told him to just put me in a foster home because I couldn't take it anymore. Thank God, he never did "get finished" with me! So, I told my mom for the last time. I decided to confront him in his denial statement that night. He kept saying that I lied and I told him: "When we all die and go to heaven and stand before Jesus, He will tell who is lying and who is telling the truth. My mom heard me say that to him. He did not touch me after that day. He did however verbally abuse me many times. For instance, one day in particular the whole family was outside. It was summer and I was on my period and my mom had bought feminine napkins for me that was too big by accident. He said, "Quit walking like you have a log or something between your legs". That was so humiliating.

In addition, when a boy would call me when I began high school, he would say things like, "I'm going to cram that phone down your throat". Come to think about it now, I guess the verbal abuse was there even before.

I kept getting worse in my depression until I didn't even talk to my friends at school anymore. I just existed, so much so that I even quit high school. Not bragging, but I was an "A" student because I threw everything I had into studying. To my great surprise, the next day after I had quit school, the school principle came to our house. He encouraged me not to quit school and talked me into going back. I am so glad that I did go back.

5

TRYING TO FIGURE IT ALL OUT

D own through the years of abuse I received from my dad, there are things I tried to figure out over and over again. I asked myself questions that I was unable to answer such as:

Why would my own father do this to me?
What was wrong with me?
Why did there seem to be two sets of Rules, two sides
to our way of life, and two parts of him?

From the beginning at three or four years of age, I hated what he did to me. I do not understand why but I did not hate him. I wanted a "normal" father/daughter relationship with him so much. I would even go so far as to say that I craved that relationship until the day he died. Maybe it was how much my mother seemed to adore him and obey his every command that caused this, I don't know. Everything she did was geared to serve him, honor him; whatever she was doing you could count on it being for him and all about him. There was a six-year age difference and my mother was only fifteen when the two of them married and he would have been about 21 years old and divorced. Many times as my siblings and I grew up, my dad treated my mom like a child. I don't know if she looked up to him as a father figure or not. In her later years, she did not do every single thing he told her but close. I couldn't help but wonder if in fact he had himself been sexually abused after learning that those things pass down through generations. There was only one clue I got for that theory when I was about ten years old. I sat next to one of my dad's uncles and he put his arm around me and began stroking my shoulder in a way that felt so wrong and bad. I quickly pulled away, got up and sat somewhere else.

When I got older, I felt like I was being punished for some defect or cursed because I was a girl. Sometimes I even regretted that I had been born female. Not only was my own *supposed to be father* sexually abusing me, I had several male cousins, of whom touched me inappropriately. They all were 8 to 10 years older than me. Perhaps some of that abuse was adolescent experimentation but not all of it was. The oldest male cousin crossed the line. When I would spend the night with my aunt, this one guy always woke me up sucking on my five-year-old bare crouch. It hurt so much and I couldn't get him to stop. Of course, by then I was thoroughly familiar with the "codes of silence; don't tell routine". I didn't tell anyone but I did cry to sleep with my aunt or for my aunt to sleep with me. She didn't know what was happening. When my aunt would lie down beside me I felt secure enough to fall asleep, only to awaken with the same painful 'leech' latched onto my private parts.

Just to explain what he did as far as discipline on the part of him that I saw as a parent:

An incident occurred at my paternal grandparents' home that I remember vividly. They used a box window fan to cool their living room, which happened to be on one day when we were visiting. I accidentally discovered that speaking into the rapid blades that turned made a sound turning my voice into such a cool sound. He noticed me playing near it and told me to stay away from it. I disobeyed because I couldn't resist hearing my distorted voice as I continued to talk into the fan. He promptly slapped my behind with his leather belt and told me to sit on the couch until he said I could get up. He never beat any of us kids and always demanded obedience and respect. Most of the time he acted as though nothing was going on as far as the abuse, and that really confused me. On the one hand, he treated me as an adult when it came to his sexual pleasures, then all other times in no uncertain terms I was treated like a kid that obeyed, respected, worked around the house, etc. For example, one day him, my brother, sister, and me went somewhere in the car and I was allowed to sit up front in momma's place because she was at work. I sat on my knees so I would appear taller and in my mind was trying to tell someone, anyone that he was making me do my mother's job in the bedroom (at least, that's what my young brain imagined). I would sing hymns in the car also in an attempt to make him listen to God's word in song. I hoped it would make him feel ashamed and stop because it was wrong. But then a horrible thought entered my mind: what if he thought I was singing because I was happy? I stopped singing to him. It seemed there was no way out...no way out.

I hated it so bad. I knew it was wrong. He knew it was wrong; otherwise he would not have threatened me if I told anyone, and then denied it when he was confronted with the truth. And yet, he kept on and on and on. I can't express enough how much I hated it. I use to just be listening to the folks talk all the time and cringe whenever I heard words indicating my mom would plan to find a job when he didn't have one. That was ongoing. In addition, there were two more things that happened to turn me into a nervous wreck. My mother always had a nervous condition and I'm sure at times she was stressed out to the max. However, one time a preacher lady came to visit my mother and talk to her and found that she did indeed need a break from us kids once in awhile as all mothers do. So... the preacher lady proposed that she come pick up my mom once in awhile and that they spend a day together just letting my mom have a little "me" time which almost made me have a nervous breakdown... and I couldn't tell the preacher lady why but I remember begging my mom to please, please not go. The preacher lady tried to explain to me why this would be so beneficial to my mom's health and happiness but she didn't know that it would doom me to a hell filled day. I felt bad about being selfish, but not enough to not beg my mom not to go and she didn't to my relief.

The most devastating incident was when I was in high school room thinking about the possibility of my mother dying and leaving me forever there with him alone and at his mercy. My mother was having surgery around that time and that is the trigger for that thinking. My heart just sunk and broke and I cried and cried and begged the Lord not to take her please. I prayed so hard and I knew God understood my selfishness.

I was so scared and at the same time so curious to know if this was happening to my cousin also that I mustered up the courage to ask her if her dad ever did anything to her or touched her at night. I knew I was right believing this was wrong when I received her answer and it was "no". At least I knew that all dads did not do these things to their daughters. My heart ached because now I wondered why this man did not love me as a daughter. I could not figure out why, ever.

I know from experience that a child can sense when something is wrong when it happens like this. I've heard it said that that's because we, as human beings are made in God's image. I do believe that children are innocent. I was a child and he was an adult. I learned that none of these things was my fault. But knowing something in your head and feeling it in your heart takes a great deal of healing. Jesus said in His word of children, *"...Let the children come to me. Don't stop them! For the Kingdom of Heaven belongs to those who are like these children."NLT Matthew 19:14*

I am certain that God was always with me. I was given many ways to cope with what was going on in my life. I do not know why I had to endure such evil things for eleven years. I do know that God is not to blame. The blame lies with man and his choices. My dad (NOT) for whatever reason made the wrong choices concerning that part of his and in this case my life. I realize that people get tired of hearing that at the appointed time, all things will be explained to us. The 'whys' will be finally be revealed to us all. I choose to trust God that it was either necessary to allow this to happen to me or either He wanted my character to be formed in a fashion that I might in some way reflect His mercy, goodness, and great love. As horrible as the whole experience has been and as negatively it has impacted my whole life, I would much rather have gone through it and had Jesus than to have not had it and not have known my Savior. He knows me better than I know myself. Would have I gone in a totally different and evil direction in my life and missed knowing His peace and joy? Would I have listened to His voice and saw how much He loves me? *"And we know that God causes everything to work together for the good of those who love God and are called according to his purpose for them" NLT Romans 8:28.*

I learned in therapy that in fact nothing was wrong with me. I was a child. I did not deserve this abuse. He was the adult and so was my mother. They should have kept me safe and not robbed my innocence and my childhood. I didn't even realize that my mother was so much to blame as well as him until I was in therapy. At that point, I got really angry with her. In the past I had always felt so sorry for her because of the fact that she was physically and verbally abused when she was a child. Her father was killed when she was eight years old. Her husband went out on her numerous times and hit her. In addition, she was verbally and emotionally abused. Nevertheless, I wish she had protected my sister and me from that monster. I know it was harder back in that day because there was not as much support for a single mother as there is now, but I believe if she had depended on God, we could have made it. For these reasons, it was certainly easier to forgive her than to forgive him.

6

LOOKING BACK

I wonder if I should have done anything differently. As I have heard it said many times, hindsight is 20/20. Only God knows what would have happened should I have made different decisions. I absolutely wish that I had not treated my parents as family after I married. I wish I had 'divorced' them. I suppose anything you do in life could have been done better and wiser. I kept thinking in my mind all of my adult life of the Ten Commandments — or rather Honor thy father and thy mother in this particular case. I did not know how to live without them. I cannot change anything now anyway. I wanted to please God with my life. I don't know if this is an excuse or a reason. God knows.

I kept thinking and hoping and praying for him to finally admit what he had done to me. In addition, I wanted him to apologize and at least give me the remnants of an earthly father. That never happened. I consider this selfishness on my part looking back.

I would also like to take this time to share some good things that have happened in my life. I married a man that loved me. He has supported me and loved me through good times and bad. He has endured my altered life as a survivor of child sexual abuse. It has not been easy but it has been worth it. We have been married nearly forty-four years this October. I wish I could have given him the wife he deserved. I feel as though God gave my husband to me. I have never felt more loved than when I married him. I am truly blessed.

God gave us two beautiful daughters. They brought lots of joy in both our lives. I only wish I could have given them the mother they deserved. I guess I have to forgive myself too.

Our beautiful granddaughter was born nearly sixteen years ago. I so adore her.

I have a loving heavenly Father that is kind and good and perfect. I am not perfect and this world is not perfect. I realize that people make mistakes, make bad choices, and hopefully repent and accept Jesus as their Savior. Becoming a child of God does not erase the consequences of what has been done, however. Certain laws of nature will not be broken until the day when God destroys this whole mess and provides a new heaven and a new earth. I look forward to that day when there will be no more pain, no more tears, or no more sorrow forever.

Until that day, I suppose unless God sees fit to completely heal me, I will have this with which to deal. People tell me that they hope that I will be able to "let it go". Even a trained Psychologist recently made the comment, "Why would you let this monster, who took your childhood continue to make you miserable"? I'm trying to explain that I do not LET that happen. The point is that I don't keep hanging on to the abuse, but rather the abuse keeps hanging onto me. At the beginning of this book, I have explained how I get filled with rage and bent out of shape and I don't even catch why I get that way! Please understand that is one of the many harmful and hurtful effects this abuse leaves. It is there. I do NOT want to keep dwelling on this. I want it to be over! I do not choose to think about it, it is just there. I pray God sees fit to take the remnants away. If He does not,

I know it will be a tool for me to use to help others. I choose to trust Him and cling to Him. I will continue to survive and if you have had similar things happen, you can survive also. If you need help, please don't hesitate to ask for help. Do not ever give up! The Bible says in Romans 8:31 *"What shall we say about such wonderful things as these? If God is for us, who can ever be against us?"* NLT! I believe Him. I know that I know that God has always been with me, helping me through. This life is worth living just because of my God and my Savior!

> *"Even if my father and mother abandon me, the LORD will hold me close."*

> *Psalms 27:10 NLT*

> *"No eye has seen, no ear has heard, and no mind has imagined what God has prepared for those who love him."*

> *I Corinthians 2:9 NLT*

7

A SECOND LOOK BACK

I am using a pen name to protect my daughters' and my husband's privacy. I was born and grew up in a small town in Western Kentucky. I do not wish to cause any more harm to them than has already been done. I lost my younger daughter in a horrible accident in the 90's. I remember trying to pray for her on my way to find her. My prayers seemed to bounce off the insides of the vehicle. In my heart, I didn't think God would take her from me because I had already been through so much during my lifetime. But the Bible tells us that God is no respecter of persons. It also says that God won't put more on us than we are able to bear. Let me tell you something, we can bear a lot more (with God's help) than we think we can. God is faithful and will never leave us alone. Nevertheless, all time in the past is divided with me. It either happened before or after my precious daughter went to heaven.

In addition, I have to tell you that as horrible as my childhood, was God helped me through it. I don't know what I would have gotten into if I hadn't had this to go through. Sometimes I think something more horrible could have happened. Only God knows the answer to that. I am not saying that I am perfect by no means. I am not. I have made so many mistakes in my life....messed up so many times. Sometimes when I have prayed, I have just asked to hide behind my Savior and let Him go before me. I believe He has done this so many times. I realize that Jesus is the only One human that has been perfect.

I also lost my sister when I was eight years old. I guess I should say that my family lost my sister in April of 1962. She was stabbed by my mentally handicapped uncle. I have always believed that my uncle meant to stab me instead of my sister. God had other plans I suppose. She was only six years old. It seemed to me that everyone loved her. I know she was very pretty. I was at times jealous of her but I loved her.

My mother told me that I was a strong willed toddler. That reminds me of my younger daughter. She always wanted to be independent. She dressed herself at two years old. She was very determined in what she wanted throughout her short life. She had a heart for helping others early on. She had the most beautiful smile. Her laughter lit up a room. She gave her daddy and me so much joy.

Our older daughter grew up helping mom with little sister. She was a daddy's girl. She never cared much for Barbie dolls, but given a small motorized car and she was elated. She and her dad raced those cars and brought home some trophies! She had a laugh so beautiful and I loved to listen to her. Praise God she still has that wonderful laugh that I love so much. Even now, all grown up she loves fishing and hunting and is quite good at it I might add. She brought us much joy also and continues to make our hearts overflow! Yes, God is so good and has blessed us with our girls and our lives.

It hasn't been easy, but all the struggles have been so worth it. God has always provided and made a way when there seemed to be no way. We have never been hungry and have always had a home. Living with a survivor of child sexual abuse is not an ideal situation to say the least. There have been so many times that I didn't even like living with myself. But I believe my husband was given to me by the

Lord Himself. You see, when my love was born the doctor delivered him and threw him over on the bed believing the infant was stillborn. But the nurse happened to see this sweet baby's hand twitch. They began to work with him and he lived. Praise be to God and the Great Physician because God knew how much I needed him.

Some forty-four years ago, I asked the Lord to show me if this was the man that I should marry. "Lord", I said, "I have to be sure". I had read stories about how God really talks to His people and answers them. Also, I had read in the Bible about a prophet putting out a fleece to be sure not to misunderstand a very important answer to a very important question. So, I said to God, "Dear God, if this is the one I'm supposed to marry please let him tell me this particular verse from the Bible". I had a verse all picked out and I did not say a word to anyone else about it. Well, that night my beau and I went out on a date. On the way home that night, we were just about back to my house where he would say goodnight. He said the exact verse I had chosen without any prompting or clues ....nothing. Just right out of the blue, he said it. Has the marriage been perfect? No. Neither of us has been perfect either. I love this guy with all my heart even more than when we first started. I believe he loves me that much too. We have learned to communicate our feelings to one another. That is so important, along with mutual respect and honesty.

At this point in my life I have looked back over my past. I do not deserve such love and mercy that I have found in my heavenly Father. He brought me through all my life's sorrows. I thank Him for helping understand that He is not to blame for what is wrong in this life. When God saved my soul, I began to read His word. I have learned that God loves each one of us with an everlasting love. His mercy and grace is so life giving. His laws are not written to beat us over the head. He genuinely cares what happens to us. If we follow His rules and laws, we are so bettered for that. Those laws are good laws that protect us and our future. They are for our good. God tells us the truth. It is the enemy who furnishes all the lies, the envy, the jealousy, the hate. The Bible tells us that God wants all to be saved. He wants only good for us….so much good in fact that no eyes have seen, no ears have heard, nor nothing has ever entered man's imagination, the good things God has in store for those who love Him. (That is paraphrased from a Bible *verse, Corinthians 2:9 NLT.*)

I want to please God with my life. I want to be the person He wants me to be in everything I do, in every area of my life. God's mercy and grace is so good and endless. I am so thankful to be a child of the most high God!

www.ingramcontent.com/pod-product-compliance
Lightning Source LLC
Chambersburg PA
CBHW060656280326
41933CB00012B/2207